What Was the Great Chicago Fire?

by Janet B. Pascal

illustrated by Tim Foley

Grosset & Dunlap
An Imprint of Penguin Random House

For Larry Bliquez—JBP

For Keenan and Tom, be careful with matches—TF

GROSSET & DUNLAP
Penguin Young Readers Group
An Imprint of Penguin Random House LLC

The publisher does not have any control over and does not assume any responsibility for author or third-party websites or their content.

Text copyright © 2016 by Janet B. Pascal. Illustrations copyright © 2016 by Penguin Random House LLC. All rights reserved. Published by Grosset & Dunlap, an imprint of Penguin Random House LLC, 345 Hudson Street, New York, New York 10014. Who HQ™ and all related logos are trademarks owned by Penguin Random House LLC. GROSSET & DUNLAP is a trademark of Penguin Random House LLC. Printed in the USA.

Library of Congress Cataloging-in-Publication Data is available.

ISBN 9780399541582 (paperback)   10 9 8 7 6 5 4 3 2
ISBN 9780399542381 (library binding)   10 9 8 7 6 5 4 3 2 1

Contents

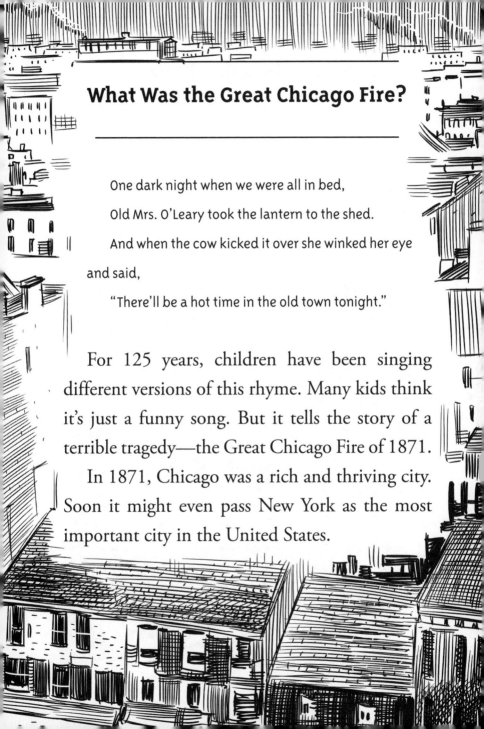

What Was the Great Chicago Fire?

One dark night when we were all in bed,

Old Mrs. O'Leary took the lantern to the shed.

And when the cow kicked it over she winked her eye and said,

"There'll be a hot time in the old town tonight."

For 125 years, children have been singing different versions of this rhyme. Many kids think it's just a funny song. But it tells the story of a terrible tragedy—the Great Chicago Fire of 1871.

In 1871, Chicago was a rich and thriving city. Soon it might even pass New York as the most important city in the United States.

Chicago leaders knew that fire was one of the main risks to a large city. So they had planned ahead. They had a top firefighting force with modern equipment. No matter how big a fire was, they were sure they could stop it.

Sadly, they were wrong.

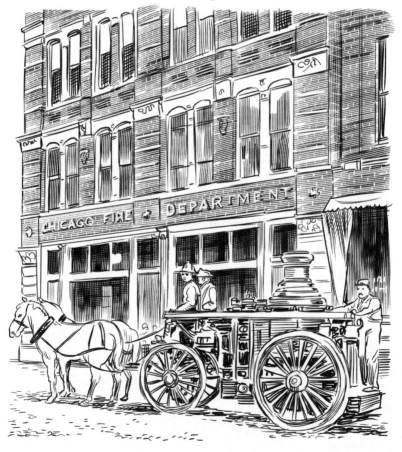

On a hot, windy October night, a fire broke out in the barn of a woman named Catherine O'Leary. The fire spread and spread for thirty hours. It jumped over two rivers. Nothing seemed to slow it down. By the time it was finally put out, most of the city was destroyed. Thousands of people, rich and poor, had lost everything.

One of the few houses that was left standing belonged to Catherine O'Leary. She and her family also survived the fire. But her cows did not. Did one of them really cause all this destruction?

CHAPTER 1
Buckets, Hoses, and Horses

Ever since people started living in houses, fire has been one of the greatest dangers they faced. For centuries most huts and cottages were made of wood or mud. Many of them had straw roofs. Inside, people used open fireplaces, candles, torches, and oil lamps for heat, light, and cooking. All this meant fires could break out at any time. And once they had started, it was easy for them to spread.

Firefighting was everyone's business. If one house caught fire, all its neighbors were in danger. As soon as anyone saw a fire, they would sound the alarm. Then everyone in the village grabbed a bucket and rushed outside. They formed a double line from the fire to the nearest pond, river, or well. They filled buckets and passed them up the line to the fire. When the bucket was empty it was passed back down the line to get filled again. This was called a bucket brigade.

As cities rose up, buildings were packed close together. Fires could spread with even greater speed. Most cities had night watchmen. They kept guard against enemies. But they also watched out for fires. They could give the alarm right away by ringing a bell.

The sooner a fire was reported, the more quickly it could be put out. The main way to fight a fire was still with buckets of water. Firefighters also chopped away wood that had not yet started burning. This took fuel away from the fire so it would die down.

Sometimes a fire was too hot to go near, or too high to reach. Then buckets and axes were not enough. In the sixteenth century, in Europe, people started to use pumps that could shoot water longer distances. The first pumps were like giant squirt guns. They were better than nothing, but they couldn't spray very far. Then around 1672, a Dutch inventor created

The first fire hose

the first fire hose. It was hand-sewn out of leather. With a hose, firefighters could aim at a blaze many feet away, and then force water through the hose at it.

Machines for fighting fires began to appear about the same time. These each had a container full of water and a pump to force it through the hose to the fire. The first ones were called hand tubs, because they had to be filled by hand and then carried to the fire. After that the water was pumped through the hose by hand.

The first fire-engine pump

A big improvement came with the invention of a machine that pulled water directly from a well or pond or other source of water. Then, in 1829, a steam pump for fighting fire was invented. Now people didn't have to pump the water by hand.

At first the heavy pumps had to be carried. Soon they were put on wheels and pulled to the fire by firefighters. It may seem odd that the men would bother dragging it themselves. Why not use a horse?

There were problems with making horses pull the engines. It took time to lead horses from their stable and harness them. And only a very special kind of horse could be used. It had to be strong and fast. Most important, it had to be brave enough to run toward a fire instead of away from it. And it had to stand still, right next to the fire while it was being put out. Most firemen didn't trust horses to do this.

Engines grew bigger and heavier, however, in the nineteenth century. Finally there was no choice. Horses were necessary. In New York City, a horse was first used to pull fire engines in 1832. It took almost thirty more years for fire horses to become common. They were carefully chosen and

trained. The city of Detroit actually established a "horse college" with report cards for each horse. The firemen worked closely with their horses, and they became very attached to each other.

Horses got so good at their job that it was sometimes hard for them to stop. After they were too old to pull fire engines, some were sold to pull wagons on city streets. At times when a fire alarm sounded, a former firehorse would try to go back to its old life. It would take off for the fire, dragging its driver along.

Dalmatians

As firefighters began using horses, Dalmatians were also added to the team. These large spotted white dogs were bred to get along with horses. When a fire alarm rang, the dogs would bark to alert the horses. Sometimes they led them out to the engines. Then the dogs ran beside the engine to the fire. Then they helped keep the horses calm and guarded the engines.

Dalmatians are not needed in modern firehouses. But if you visit a station, you'll see that many still keep one as a pet.

CHAPTER 2
Firefighters

Originally all firefighters were volunteers. They offered their services for free. By fighting a fire in a neighbor's house, they were helping themselves, too. But there were drawbacks with volunteers. There might not be enough people in the area when a fire broke out. Lazy or scared people might not help. And firefighting equipment was getting more complicated. People had to be trained in how to use it.

By the eighteenth century, volunteer brigades were no longer able to keep big cities safe. When a fire broke out near the capitol building in Williamsburg, Virginia, an eyewitness described complete chaos. No one knew where the nearest water supply was. They couldn't find buckets and ladders. People got in each other's way. No one was directing the operation.

So cities started to organize volunteers into groups and train them. One pioneer in this movement was Benjamin Franklin. In 1735, he

Benjamin Franklin

wrote that for every fire engine in the city, there should be a "Club or Society of active Men . . . whose Business is to attend all Fires with it whenever they happen." Soon Philadelphia had several volunteer firemen's clubs. Their members met between fires to learn new methods.

The idea spread to other cities. Important men wanted to belong to a firemen's club. It was a good place to meet useful people or start a career in politics. As they trained together, many club members formed strong, close bonds. When the Civil War began in 1861, entire fire companies joined up together to fight as a unit.

Sadly, some firefighters started to see their group as a kind of sports team. They wanted their own group to put out a fire, not any other group. Teams tried to stop others from getting there first. A team might block off a water source so that no one else could use it. Or one man might go ahead and then fight off any teams that arrived before his own.

Some buildings had fire insurance. If they caught fire, the insurance company would pay the building owner for what he lost. They would also reward the volunteer company that put out the fire. Buildings with insurance coverage

usually posted a metal sign from the insurance
company on the wall. Sometimes several engine
companies would fight for the right to save an
insured building. Meanwhile, a building next to
it that was also burning but not insured would
be ignored.

By the middle of the nineteenth century,
battles between volunteer firefighting companies

were a real problem. Some cities decided that it would be better for the local government to hire and pay firefighters. In 1853, Cincinnati, Ohio, became the first city in the United States with a professional firefighting system. Five years later, Chicago became one of several cities to follow suit.

Firefighters in Ancient Rome

The world's first firefighting company was started around 100 BCE by a citizen of ancient Rome named Marcus Crassus. When a fire broke out, he and his slaves would show up. Marcus would offer to buy the burning property—at a bargain price. If the owner would not sell, Marcus would tell his men to let the building burn. Then they would offer a lower price. They would watch the fire destroy the building and keep offering less and less money, until the owner got so desperate that he agreed to a very low price. Then the slaves would put out the fire. Marcus became one of the richest men in Roman history.

Marcus Licinius Crassus

CHAPTER 3
The Center of the Country

Chicago is one of the younger cities in the United States. Fort Dearborn was built on the site in 1803. A town quickly grew up around it. In 1837, Chicago officially became a city. About four thousand people lived there. It grew so fast that by 1871, it had three hundred thousand people.

Fort Dearborn

What was the reason for Chicago's success? Its location.

The nation was spreading out across the North American continent. Farmers were settling the rich land of the prairie. Smart businessmen saw that Chicago sat in the perfect spot to link the new western farms with the old cities of the East. The city sits on the farthest southwestern point of the Great Lakes. These are five lakes as big as

seas, linked to each other. They stretch all the way to New York State. In the 1820s, the Erie Canal had been built. It connected the Great Lakes to the Hudson River, which flowed into New York City. In 1848, another canal opened. It connected Chicago to the Mississippi River, which runs all the way south to the Gulf of Mexico. From Chicago, cargo could be moved by boat almost anywhere in the settled parts of the United States.

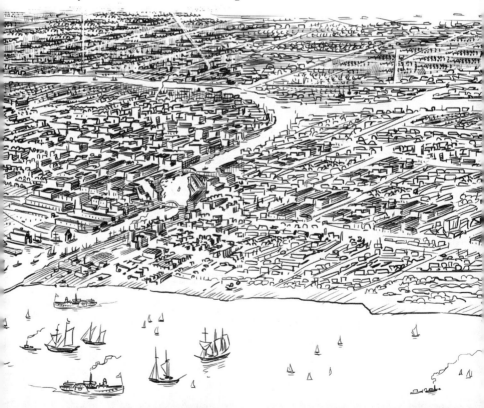

For this reason, most railroads connecting the East and West went through Chicago. By 1871, twenty-one different main railroad lines ran to the city. They brought grain that was stored in huge silos. Cattle were driven from farms all over the West to huge stockyards in Chicago. Then the cattle were killed, and the meat was shipped east. In the year of the fire, over three million heads of cattle came to the Chicago stockyards.

The Wheeler Mansion

Chicago was the fastest-growing city in the whole country. Rich people in Chicago wanted elegant homes and offices and churches. This would show they were just as sophisticated as the cities back east. So they designed buildings that looked as if they were made of stone, with fancy carvings and copper spires. But they weren't made of stone. North of Chicago were huge virgin forests. Wood was cheap and easy to get. So almost everything was built of wood. Then it was painted to look like stone, marble, or copper. Even the streets were paved with wooden blocks cut into the shape of bricks.

Chicago had a big problem with mud. That was because it was built right on the shore of Lake Michigan. A lot of the land was originally swamp. Every spring the mud was so deep that people sank into it. There was a popular joke about a Chicago man who saw a traveler sunk into the mud up to his neck. "Are you all right?" the man asked. "I'm fine," the traveler said. "I'm riding on a good horse."

Citizens decided they had to do something about the mud. So they lifted the whole city up several feet. Sidewalks were raised on top of

wooden poles. Important buildings were moved
up using a kind of big screw. Slowly it lifted the
building out of its foundations. The method
worked so well that one hotel was raised several
feet while the guests were still in it. No one felt
a thing.

Another problem for the city was water. Most of the water people used came from the muddy Chicago River. People complained that little fish sometimes came out with the water. So in 1867, the city built a magnificent new waterworks. A tunnel ran two miles out into Lake Michigan. It drew water all the way into the city. A tall water tower created pressure so a pumping station could send water through pipes to the whole city.

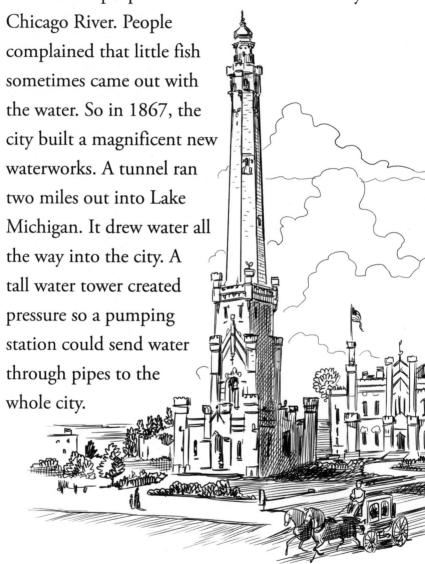

Chicago also set up one of the best fire systems in the country. Their firemen were well paid and trained. As well as regular fire engines, the city owned seventeen of the newest steam pump engines. These were powerful enough to

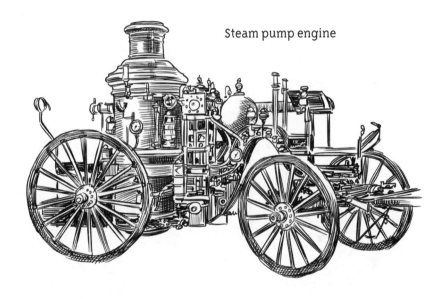

Steam pump engine

send water a long distance. Fire trucks could be hooked up to water plugs connected to the new waterworks system. This meant they could use all of Lake Michigan to help put out a fire.

Most important of all, an alarm system was put in place to help firemen get to a fire quickly. Every firehouse had its own watchman. There was also a central watchman in the high tower of the central courthouse. He could watch for fires

Chicago's central courthouse

anywhere in the city. Telegraph boxes all around the city could send an alarm to the central tower. Then the courthouse watchman would telegraph the fire stations that were nearest to the fire, so they could get there right away.

People in Chicago were very proud of their city and the way it solved problems. They called it the Garden City and the Gem of the Prairie.

Map of Chicago

From Lake Michigan, the Chicago River runs east to west for about a mile. Then it splits into a T shape. One branch stretches up to the north, the other down to the south. This divides the city into three main parts. Below the east-to-west river is the South Side. This held most of the businesses, offices, and hotels, as well as the older slums. Above the east-to-west river is the North Side, where many rich people had their houses. On the other side of the river branches is the West Side. Many working-class immigrants lived in this area. There were also a lot of factories. There is no East Side—if there were, it would be in the lake.

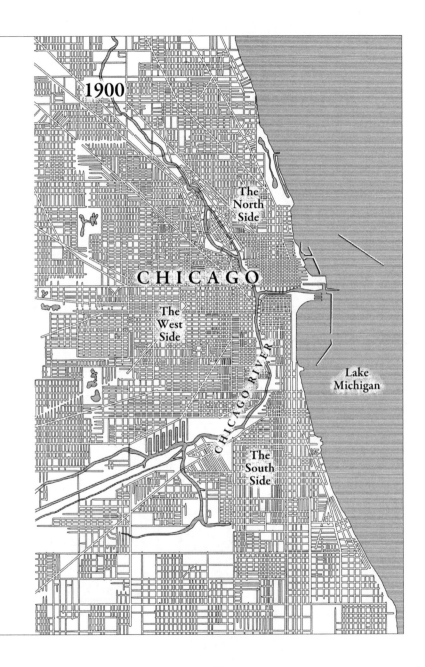

1900

CHICAGO

The
North
Side

The
West
Side

The
South
Side

CHICAGO RIVER

Lake
Michigan

CHAPTER 4
A Disaster Waiting to Happen

The summer of 1871 was unusually dry and hot around Chicago. Between July and October, there was almost no rain. Everything was so dry, the smallest spark could start a fire. They broke out every day. A special patrol was set up to walk the city streets. They carried chemical fire extinguishers. They put out every small fire before it could become a big one.

In Chicago, it was easy for a fire to get out of hand. So much of the city was made of wood. And the raised wooden sidewalks were hollow underneath. They created tunnels that a fire could race through to spread to new areas. Mixed in with houses and offices were small factories. They used materials like paint and coal that burned rapidly. The whole city was one big collection of fuel. The *Chicago Tribune* warned that "a spark might set a fire which would sweep from end to end of the city."

On October 7, a lecturer came to Chicago. He warned that "a terrible calamity" was about to destroy the city. Sure enough, that very evening,

a fire broke out in the West Side. This area had lumberyards full of sawdust, a paper box factory, and many saloons. The insurance patrol had a nickname for the West Side—"the red flash." That was because it would go up in flames so easily.

The fire department came right away. But everything was so dry that the fire burned fiercely. A second alarm was sounded, and then a third, calling for more help. It began to look as if the firefighters were going to lose. People who lived in houses nearby brought out their furniture and piled it in the streets. That way, if they had to flee, they could take their possessions with them. But blowing cinders from the fire set the furniture alight and helped spread the flames. Firemen fought so close to the blazing heat that their eyes swelled shut. Some of them were injured. Their equipment also suffered. One steamer was damaged, and one firehouse

collapsed. Four entire city blocks and a railroad bridge were destroyed. It was the biggest fire Chicago had ever seen.

But in the end, the firemen won. They stopped the fire before it could sweep through their city and destroy it. They had proved that their firefighting system worked. Now they could go home and recover.

CHAPTER 5
Mrs. O'Leary's Shed

Sunday, October 8, was a day of rest for the weary firemen. The day was hot and clear, with gusting wind.

The area just south of Saturday's fire was a neighborhood of Irish immigrants. In a small wooden house, Patrick and Catherine O'Leary lived with their children. He worked as a laborer.

She kept five cows and a calf and sold their milk. Both of them went to bed early that night. They had to be up at five to milk the cows and get ready for work.

They rented half their house to another man. He was having a party that night, to celebrate the arrival of a relative from Ireland. Daniel "Peg Leg" Sullivan, who had a wooden leg, had been visiting in the neighborhood and was now sitting outside.

Daniel "Peg Leg" Sullivan

Around 8:30, Peg Leg saw flames shooting out of the O'Learys' barn. He cried out, "Fire, fire!" and ran into the barn to save the cows. Flames shot up so fast that he was afraid he wouldn't get out again. He fell, and his wooden leg came off. Fortunately he was able to set the calf free. He wrapped his arms around its neck and let it drag him out of the barn.

This is all we know for sure. A newspaper reporter wrote that the fire was Mrs. O'Leary's fault. He described her as an old, lazy, dirty woman who didn't care when a cow kicked a lamp over. At that time there was a lot of prejudice against

Irish immigrants. So people found this story easy to believe. However, it was not true. Catherine O'Leary was in her early forties, hardworking, and smart. She later proved that she was already in bed before the fire started. The reporter had to admit he had made up the whole story.

Some people think maybe Peg Leg Sullivan started the fire. He could have gone into the barn for some reason and knocked over a lamp. When he saw fire, perhaps he lied about rushing in from outside. Another story goes that the neighbor's friends were drinking and playing cards in the barn, and they knocked over a candle.

We will never know for sure what started the fire. But we do know that it spread very quickly. The O'Learys got their children outside. Their house was just south of the burning barn. They began to pour water on it to save it. The wind

was blowing hard, but it was blowing the fire north, away from the house. So the O'Learys' house survived. But everything north of it was in danger. The fire raced along wooden fences and blew from building to building.

One of the O'Learys' neighbors went to do the right thing—send in a fire alarm. When a fire is spreading, every minute counts. While it's still small and in one place, it is easy to put out. But within minutes it can become huge and hard to handle. The nearest fire alarm box was at Goll's drugstore. It was three blocks away. So the neighbor ran to the drugstore. That was the last thing anyone would do right for a long time.

CHAPTER 6
"Everything Went Wrong"

Later on, one firefighter said sadly, "From the beginning of that fatal fire, everything went wrong." The fire alarm box at the drugstore was kept locked so people couldn't send in false alarms. When the neighbor asked Goll to unlock it, Goll said no. It wasn't worth the trouble. He had just seen a fire truck go by. He figured the firefighters were already on the way. There was no need for an alarm. Unfortunately, he was wrong. No fire truck was on the way.

In the center of the city, a watchman was on duty in the courthouse tower. He had some visitors with him. One of them saw smoke and pointed it out to him. But the O'Learys' barn was right behind the area that had burned down the day before. So the watchman told his visitors not to worry. The smoke was just left over from yesterday's fire.

A little later he looked again and saw flames shooting into the sky. He realized he had been wrong. He immediately sent an alarm to the stations nearest the fire. But he guessed wrong about where the fire was. He sent the fire engines to a place a mile away. The next time he looked out, he realized his mistake. He told his assistant to

cancel the old alarm and send out a new one with the right location. But his assistant didn't do it. He thought it would cause confusion. He thought that the firemen would see where the fire really was without being told.

While all these mistakes were being made, important time was lost. Finally a few firefighters arrived with two engines. They had just spent

sixteen hours fighting the fire the day before. They were tired and had not had time to recover. Both engines were old and not very powerful. The new steam engines that could direct a strong stream of water were still going to the imaginary fire a mile away.

The fire started spreading north along one
street and east along another at the same time. It
was much too big for two small fire trucks to fight.
The men had to get very near the fire in order to
reach it with their hoses. By now it was hot enough
to burn anyone standing that close. They did their

best. They stayed near the fire as long as they could stand it. Then they'd move back to recover until they could go back to fight some more. Some of them tried to use doors from the burned buildings to shield themselves from the heat. But the air was so hot that the doors burst into flames.

Finally the chief fire marshal arrived with the modern steam engines. He ordered his men to surround the fire. However, there weren't enough of them. So he sent someone to call in a second alarm asking for more engines. This fireman ran to the fire alarm box at Goll's Drugstore—the same place as before. This time an alarm was sent. But he made a mistake. He used the wrong code. At the courthouse, they thought the fireman was just telling them where the fire was, not asking for more help.

It looked as if there was no way to stop the fire from destroying the next fifteen or sixteen blocks. Then it would reach the four blocks that had already been burned the day before. Beyond that was the river. This was good news. This large, empty space with nothing left to burn should stop the fire. If not, the river itself would. Or so people thought.

CHAPTER 7
Across the River

Chicago was proud of its new firefighting equipment. But it had seen hard use during the fire the night before. It was worn out, and some of it needed work. The firefighters had been too tired to fix it after the fire.

Now some of it was starting to break down. Hoses burst open. A few of them actually started to burn. Some steam engines stopped working.

All this time, the wind was blowing harder and harder. And heat from the fire created its own wind that swirled as fast as a tornado. A spark flew all the way up to the steeple of Saint Paul's Church. This was one of the highest points in the West Side. From so high up, the fire could be blown almost anywhere. Right near the church were several lumberyards full of wood and sawdust,

and a factory that made matches. These all blazed up at once. Burning pieces of wood sailed high into the sky.

People across the river in the heart of the city thought they were safe. Many of them went out to watch the fire as though it were an exciting play. One man called it, "such a view, such a magnificent sight!" But they were wrong. They were not safe. Cinders from the church steeple flew all the way to the South Side and set it alight.

The fire had crossed the river.

Soon flames were spreading through the South Side faster than a man could run. People suddenly realized they only had a few minutes to escape. One woman was giving birth. She and her baby were carried out on a stretcher minutes after he was born.

People grabbed the few things they valued most, and ran. A thirteen-year-old girl put on all her best clothing, one piece over another.

A six-year-old ran back into her house at the last minute to grab a beloved doll. Some people were practical. They took food, clothes, and bedding. Others took items they couldn't bear to lose: the family Bible, paintings of relatives, a dead child's toys. In the confusion of the moment, many people didn't know what to rescue. One woman ran into the street with her frying pan and muffin tins. Others carried things like a feather duster or an armload of umbrellas.

Many people wanted to save their pets. One little girl carried a box with four puppies. A boy led his pet goat on a leash. One woman clutched a huge birdcage. Out of habit, people carefully locked the doors before they left their doomed houses, and put their keys in their pockets.

Some families brought their furniture and belongings down to the street. The lucky ones had their own carts. The rest had to hire one. Carts suddenly became very expensive. Drivers asked as much as ten times their usual price. They had to be paid in cash right then and there, or they would go find someone else. And if they were offered more money, they might dump one family's load and replace it with another's.

More generous drivers carried whole families and their goods for free. Some of them then went back into the fire to rescue more people.

Men ran to their offices to get important books and papers. Many rescued cash, shares of stock, and records belonging to their clients. After the fire, some families were saved from ruin because a clerk had risked his life to save papers they would need.

In order to help, some people kept working until the last possible moment. The telegraph operator stayed so long, he had to stop sending his final message in the middle of a sentence. Workers at the post office raced to load all the mail on wagons and send it to safety. Volunteers at the railroad depot pushed more than a hundred loaded freight cars down the tracks and out of danger by hand. Newspapermen at the *Chicago Times* office tried to publish one final edition. The last article they wrote said, "The entire business portion of the city is burning up, and the TIMES building is doomed." Then they ran.

"The Windy City"

Strong wind was one of the main reasons the Chicago fire spread so fast. And the most popular nickname for Chicago is "the Windy City." But the nickname probably refers to another kind of wind. The rest of the country thought politicians in Chicago bragged about their city too much. In the nineteenth century, *wind* was a slang term for empty boasts. People called Chicago "the Windy City" to make fun of it. In 1892, a newspaper reporter wrote that once people saw Chicago, they stopped joking. They discovered that everything Chicago bragged about was really true.

CHAPTER 8
Escape

Once people escaped their houses, they were still not safe. The streets were a nightmare. The air was so full of hot ash that one witness said, "It was like a snowstorm, only the flakes were red instead of white." Where the streets were paved with wood, the ground itself was burning.

Heat from the fire blew burning chunks of buildings wildly in all directions. Family members separated from one another in the confusion.

One important question was on everyone's mind. How far would the fire go? Where could they escape to? No one could go south. The fire

blocked them in that direction. Some people
headed east to the lake and gathered on the
beach. But the fire quickly burned all the way to
the shore. To survive, people had to wade out into
the water up to their necks.

To the north and west, the Chicago River could be crossed only by bridges and tunnels. One by one, these caught fire. Those that were left were quickly choked with people trying to escape. The bridges were so crowded that people were pushed

off into the water. Some bridge keepers stayed at their posts until it was too late to escape. They were trying to keep the bridges from catching fire so as many people as possible could cross.

The heat bent and melted the iron framework
of the bridges. Ships on the river were trapped
behind them. Even though they were on the water,

they weren't safe. The ships were built of wood and burned quickly. Oil on the surface of the water caught fire. Soon, even the river itself was burning.

Some new buildings downtown had proudly claimed that they were fireproof. They were built of stone, with nowhere for a fire to catch hold. People stayed in them, feeling safe. But the roofs were just wood covered with tar. Burning cinders were flying so high that the roofs caught fire. Then the flames traveled down the wooden staircases. Not one of the "fireproof" buildings survived.

A prison was located on the bottom floor of the courthouse. Some people tried to break down the door. They thought the prisoners locked up inside would be burned alive. But an official stopped them. He said the prisoners should stay. They would be safe because the building was fireproof. What was more, if anyone broke the door down, the city would make them pay for a new one. Finally the mayor ordered the prisoners to be freed. As they left, they passed a jewelry shop. The owner had saved everything he could. He told the newly liberated prisoners that they might as well take any of the jewels that were left. Otherwise they would just burn.

The watchman in the courthouse tower stayed as long as possible. When he had to leave, he left the huge bell ringing. It continued to sound the alarm until the tower collapsed and the bell was destroyed. After the fire, the metal from the bell was saved. It was used to make little bells and fire-hat charms that were sold as souvenirs.

CHAPTER 9
Camping in the Cemetery

Many people who escaped from the South Side fled to buildings on the North Side. They believed the fire wouldn't be able to cross the main branch of the river. But it was completely out of control. The firefighters tried every trick they could think of. One city official wanted to blow up buildings to stop the fire in its tracks. He didn't have any experience doing this. But eventually he got permission to try it at the edge of the South Side. This may have helped save a

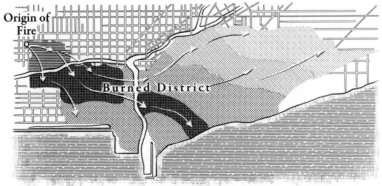

The route of the fire

few blocks. But by now the wind was so strong that nothing could hold in the fire. Sparks and cinders blew as far as two miles through the air. The North Side had no chance. By 2:30 in the morning it, too, was ablaze. The weary refugees had to move on again. Many of them had to leave behind whatever they had saved earlier.

Most rich people lived on the North Side. Their elegant mansions—full of books and artwork—stood in beautiful private gardens. They had more warning that the fire was coming, so they

had time to prepare. And many of them owned horses and carriages. Still, they could rescue only a small part of their treasures.

People saved things they could not carry by burying them. They dug deep pits. Then they wrapped their books, china, silver, and other heavy valuables in carpets, and covered the pits with sand. They hoped that after the fire, they

could come back and dig things up. For some this worked. But others came back and found that everything had melted.

Some North Side people simply could not believe that the fire would destroy their mansions. They stayed and sprayed water on their roofs to protect them. However, the fire was moving so fast now that a place might look safe one minute, but a few minutes later a sheet of flame would destroy the whole building. Some people didn't leave until the last second. They were lucky to survive.

About thirty thousand people fled north to Lincoln Park. This was a large, open area on the river. There were no buildings to catch fire. To get there, people had to go through two huge cemeteries. Some families spent the night camping among the gravestones.

Other people thought even Lincoln Park wasn't far enough. They were afraid the fire would keep going until it ran out of city to burn. Hundreds of families drove their carts all the way out to the prairie. Then they piled furniture in a hollow square. They covered the top with a carpet and made themselves a tent. However, even this far out,

they couldn't be sure they were safe. After weeks with no rain, the dry prairie grass was ready to burst into flames. One survivor later remembered staying awake all night as he "watched the ring of fire draw nearer."

By now it was clearly hopeless. The fire was much too big for the firefighters to surround. They had telegraphed to neighboring cities asking for help. More fire engines were on the way. But they would be too late. The city was almost destroyed. Still the firefighters never gave up. They had been working for hours. Most of them were injured, tired, and hungry. But they continued to fight, saving a building or street for as long as possible. This gave people a little more time to escape.

Lost Treasures

Some priceless pieces of history were lost in the fire. The original Emancipation Proclamation, the document in which President Abraham Lincoln freed the Southern slaves, was kept in the Chicago Historical Society's building. The elderly librarian tried his best to rescue it, but he failed. The fire moved in on him so fast that he had to jump through a burning window, and he just barely escaped.

CHAPTER 10
Finally!

Then, without warning, water stopped coming out of the hoses. The final blow had come. All this time, the splendid new Chicago Waterworks had been doing its job. Whatever other problems the firemen faced, they knew that their hoses had a whole lake full of water to use.

A Chicago store before the fire

Cook County Courthouse and City Hall before the disaster

Rendering of the Chicago Water Tower

Illustration showing Chicago in flames

Scene of destruction

The courthouse after the fire

Rubble of Trinity Church

Remains of State and Madison streets

CORNER
STATE & MADISON ST
AFTER CHICAGO FIRE

Marbles fused together by the heat

Advertisement for a rally to help Chicago fire victims

Parade for the World's Fair Columbian Exposition

Palace of Mechanic Arts at the Columbian Exposition

The Tribune Tower, an example of a skyscraper cathedral

Skyscrapers along Lake Michigan in modern-day Chicago

The Willis Tower was once the world's tallest building

The recognizable round towers of Chicago's Marina City

The Water Tower today

The fire tower and pumping station were built to be fireproof. They were made of stone. The roofs were slate, not wood. And men had been stationed there to make sure they stayed safe. Around three o'clock in the morning, a burning piece of wood twelve feet long came sailing through the air. It dropped onto the roof of the pumping station. The wooden window frames and doors began to burn. The flames found their way inside, to the wood and plaster ceilings. The pumping station was doomed. The pumps stopped working, and the pipes melted in the heat. Chicago had no more water.

The pumping station

Near the shore, fire engines could still draw water directly from Lake Michigan. But other than that, the fight was over. There was nothing anyone could do. There didn't seem to be any reason the fire would ever stop. Already it was threatening Lincoln Park, where thousands of people had found shelter. Soon it would sweep out to the prairie, where there were endless miles of grass for it to burn.

Then, at eleven at night, it began to rain. Finally!

Within a few hours, the fire was almost out. Nature managed to do what Chicago's firefighters could not. Small pockets of fire continued to burn for days or months. But finally, after thirty hours, the crisis was over.

Great Fires

At some time in their history, many of the world's cities have had a Great Fire. One of the earliest happened in Rome in the year 64. It burned for six days. Many people thought the emperor Nero set the fire on purpose so he could rebuild the city the way he wanted it.

A famous great fire broke out in London in 1666, in a baker's shop. It lasted four days and destroyed almost 80 percent of the city. It may also have helped end the Great Plague. The plague was a sickness that was killing thousands of Londoners. The Great Fire killed the rats that carried it.

Other cities that have had great fires include Munich, Amsterdam, Oslo, Copenhagen, Moscow, Montreal, Baltimore, and Houston.

London burning in 1666

CHAPTER 11
After the Fire

The rain had saved the city. But Chicago's problems were far from over. An area four miles long and almost a mile wide had been completely

destroyed. Here and there, some walls stood, but most of the city was smoking piles of rubble. People could only guess what street they were on. One little girl was separated from her family. For hours she waited patiently where she thought their house was. In the evening her father finally found her. She had sat all day on the wrong block.

More than 17,500 buildings had been destroyed. In the entire area of the fire, only seven buildings were left. No one knows exactly how many people died. It was probably around three hundred. This is less than you might expect from such a huge disaster. Even though the firefighters couldn't put out the fire, they slowed it down in places. This gave people more time to escape.

But over one hundred thousand people in the city—one out of three—were homeless. Many of them had no money, no food, and no way of getting either. Because the waterworks had burned, people could get water only from the lake or from old wells. Looters wandered the streets, looking for things to steal. Fights broke out.

The city authorities were afraid that the thousands of homeless people might be dangerous. So martial law was declared. This meant that instead of the city government running things, the army took over. Major General Philip Sheridan, a Civil War veteran, was put in charge of about a

Major General
Philip Sheridan

thousand soldiers. They kept watch over the city and question anyone found outside at night. This lasted a few weeks, until people realized that it wasn't needed. There were no lawless mobs in the city.

Rescue work started right away. By Monday night, thousands of army tents had been put up to house the homeless. The mayor set up centers to give out supplies. People from all over the world quickly sent food, clothing, and money to help victims. They also donated lumber. People were given enough material to build small shacks to live in. Women were given free sewing machines, so that they would have a way to earn a living.

The railroads gave free passes to anyone leaving the city. But most people wanted to stay and help rebuild. The day after the fire, people were already finding ways to restart their lives. The first business to reopen in the burned-out area was a woman who sold roasted chestnuts. She parked her cart right where it had always been.

Hundreds of people rushed to Chicago. Some were there to help. But many just wanted to see the site of such an enormous disaster. Children soon found out that these visitors would pay for souvenirs of the fire. They set up stands to sell things like glass marbles melted together into a giant ball or books and stacks of paper turned to charcoal. Adults earned money by setting up hotels and restaurants to serve the tourists.

Chicago residents had always bragged that their city was the best in the world. Now they bragged that their fire was the greatest ever. One proud resident wrote, "No city can equal now the ruins of Chicago."

The Great Peshtigo Fire

Chicago wasn't the only place burning on October 8, 1871. All over the Great Lakes region, the land was ready to burst into flames. In Peshtigo, Wisconsin, a fire had been lit to clear land. But it got out of control. Before it was finished, 1.2 million

acres of forest had been destroyed, along with twelve small towns. Between 1,500 and 2,500 people were killed. The fire was described as, "a wall of flame, a mile high, five miles wide, traveling 90 to 100 miles per hour." On the very same day, the Great Michigan Fire also destroyed several towns and acres of forest.

CHAPTER 12
Rebuilding

Not everybody in Chicago lost everything. Some people had fire insurance, or property outside Chicago. Before they fled their offices, businessmen put their valuable papers in vaults or safes. After the fire they went back for them. They had to be careful not to open anything while it was too hot. When air rushed into a superheated safe, everything in it immediately burned to dust. But some people were lucky. They managed to save their fortunes.

One young man wrote his father a long description of the fire. He knew it was a terrible disaster. Even so, he ended his letter, "P.S. Don't you think it would be well to take advantage of the present to invest a little money out here?" He was not alone. For anyone with money, Chicago after the fire looked like a wonderful chance to get rich. It was still right at the heart of every kind of transportation. People all over the country needed Chicago to start working again, as soon as possible.

Businesses set up temporary offices in quickly built wooden shacks. Shops opened up inside churches or house basements—wherever they could find a space. Two Chicago newspapers managed to put out special editions the very day the fire went out. The telegraph company reopened inside a warehouse. People lined up for blocks to send telegrams. They wanted to tell their

friends they had survived. For the first day, the telegrams were sent for free. Real estate offices were especially busy in the days after the fire. One real estate agent put up a sign that spoke for all the people who were grateful to have survived the fire and ready to move on. It read, "All gone but wife, children, and energy."

By the day after the fire, new buildings had started springing up everywhere. Suddenly there was a lot of work for carpenters, bricklayers,

and other laborers. Because there was so much
demand, wages were high.
Everyone was determined
that soon the city would
be as prosperous as ever.
"Chicago Shall Rise Again,"
declared one newspaper.

CHAPTER 13
The Little Chicago Fire

At first it seemed that not much had been learned from the fire. New buildings downtown were not supposed to be made of wood. But temporary wooden buildings were allowed. Many people built "temporary" buildings and just left them up. Others used wooden decorations on their stone buildings. In July 1874, another fire swept through part of downtown Chicago. It was called the Little Fire. But it wasn't all that little. About eight hundred buildings were burned.

After that, insurance companies refused to insure Chicago buildings until a strict building code was created. This led to a new kind of building. It was supported by an iron or steel frame, and covered with terra-cotta or stone.

Soon downtown Chicago was full of elegant, ornamented buildings, including the world's first skyscraper.

The Home Insurance Building

In 1893, twenty-two years after the Great Fire, Chicago hosted the largest and grandest World's Fair ever. It was called the Columbian Exposition. Chicago welcomed more than 26 million visitors from all over the world that year.

They were proud to show the world that their city
was even stronger and more beautiful than it had
been before the Great Fire.

The Chicago fire was not the last Great Fire. In 1889, the Seattle business district burned down after a pot of boiling glue was upset in a shop. In 1906, most of San Francisco was destroyed by the fires that followed a huge earthquake. But new building techniques, fire precautions, and firefighting methods were created because of the Great Chicago Fire. Today, cities are much safer. Even the most terrible fires do not usually burn out of control. We have learned how to contain fires before they can break free and destroy an entire city.

Chicago has a sense of humor about its Great Fire. On the site where Mrs. O'Leary's cow didn't kick over a lantern, the city built the Chicago Fire Academy. So today, student firemen learn how to fight fires on the very spot where the Great Fire began.

The Chicago Fire Academy

Chicago Today

After the fire, important new buildings went up in Chicago faster than anywhere else in the country. Some were beautiful old-fashioned Gothic towers that looked like skyscraper cathedrals. Others were a new kind of building. They were designed to look clean and simple, and to let in a lot of light. These buildings grew into a new school of architecture called "the Chicago School." Today Chicago is the third largest city in the United States, after New York and Los Angeles. Over 2.7 million people live there. Its airport is the busiest in the world. And it is famous for its architecture.

The Chicago Building

Timeline of Chicago, Fires, and the Great Chicago Fire

c. 100 BCE	World's first firefighting company created in Rome
64 CE	Great Fire of Rome
1666	Great London Fire
1672	Dutch inventor creates the first fire hose
1719	First documented description of a Dalmatian, the firefighter's dog
1735	Benjamin Franklin suggests all cities create volunteer fire brigades
1803	Fort Dearborn built on the site that would become Chicago
1825	Completion of the Erie Canal connects Chicago to New York by water
1829	Invention of a steam pump that could be used by fire engines
1832	First use of a horse to pull fire engines in New York
1837	Chicago officially becomes a city
1848	Illinois and Michigan Canal connects Chicago to the Mississippi River
1853	Cincinnati establishes the first professional firefighting department in the United States
1858	Chicago establishes a professional firefighting department

1867	Chicago begins work on a new water tower and pumping station
1871	Great Chicago Fire begins around 8:30 p.m. on October 8
	By the morning of October 10, the fire is mostly extinguished
1874	In July, the Little Fire destroys parts of the rebuilt Chicago
1885	World's first skyscraper built in Chicago
1889	Great Seattle Fire
1893	Chicago World's Fair: Columbian Exposition brings millions of visitors to the city
1906	San Francisco earthquake and great fire

Timeline of the World

100 BCE —	Julius Caesar is born
79 CE —	Mount Vesuvius erupts, destroying Pompeii
1649 —	King Charles I executed in England
1692 —	Salem Witch Trials begin in Massachusetts
1719 —	Pennsylvania's first newspaper published
1731 —	Benjamin Franklin establishes the first American public library in Philadelphia
1732 —	George Washington born
1803 —	Louisiana Purchase doubles the size of the United States
1825 —	World's first modern railway opens in England
1835 —	Assassin attempts to kill President Andrew Jackson
1838 —	The Cherokee Nation is forcibly relocated
1839 —	Slaves aboard the *Amistad* rebel and take control of the ship
1845–1850 —	Many poor Irish move to the United States to escape the Great Potato Famine
1848 —	A wave of revolutions breaks out in Europe, beginning in France
1861 —	Beginning of the American Civil War
1871 —	National Association of Professional Base Ball Players created

1871 —	Great Peshtigo Fire and Great Michigan Fire both destroy acres of land on October 8
1873 —	Blue jeans are patented by Levi Strauss and Jacob Davis
1883 —	Eruption of Krakatoa (present day Indonesia) kills thirty-six thousand
1886 —	Benz Patent Motorwagen, the first automobile, is introduced
1893 —	Thomas Edison builds the first movie studio, in New Jersey
1903 —	Wright brothers make first powered airplane flight

Bibliography

*Books for young readers

Bales, Richard F. *The Great Chicago Fire and the Myth of Mrs. O'Leary's Cow.* Jefferson, NC: McFarland & Company, 2002.

Cromie, Robert. *The Great Chicago Fire.* Reissue. Nashville: Rutledge Hill Press, 1994.

Lowe, David Garrard, ed. *The Great Chicago Fire: In Eyewitness Accounts and 70 Contemporary Photographs and Illustrations.* New York: Dover Publications, 1979

* McHugh, Janet. *The Great Chicago Fire.* New York: Bearport Publishing, 2007.

Miller, Ross. *American Apocalypse: The Great Fire and the Myth of Chicago.* Chicago: University of Chicago Press, 1990.

* Murphy, Jim. *The Great Fire.* New York: Scholastic, 1995.

Websites

The Great Chicago Fire and the Web of Memory.
http://www.greatchicagofire.org/web-of-memory.